SABBATH MOOD HOMESCHOOL
PRESENTS

Living Science Study Guides

A Charlotte Mason Resource for Exploring Science, a Vast and Joyous Realm

HIGH SCHOOL CHEMISTRY
PART 2

Accompanying the book *Wonders of Chemistry* by A. Frederick Collins

SMH HIGH SCHOOL CHEMISTRY: PART 2

Second Edition: July 2024
ISBN: 9798516392825

www.SabbathMoodHomeschool.com

"But for the most part science as she is taught leaves us cold; the utility of scientific discoveries does not appeal to the best that is in us, though it makes a pretty urgent and general appeal to our lower avidities. But the fault is not in science—that mode of revelation which is granted to our generation, may we reverently say?—but in our presentation of it by means of facts and figures and demonstrations that mean no more to the general audience than the point demonstrated, never showing the wonder and magnificent reach of the law unfolded."

-CHARLOTTE MASON, *TOWARDS A PHILOSOPHY OF EDUCATION.*

Introduction

This is part two of a three-part course in high school chemistry. In this study guide, students will be introduced to the principles and tools of the study of chemistry. They will learn about gunpowder and fireworks, the chemical makeup of plants, nitrogen fixation, photosynthesis, and the invention of fertilizer. They will also learn the similarities and differences between natural rubber, fiber, and color pigments and their laboratory prepared counterparts, even making several themselves. Finally, they will learn several ways humans capture the sun's energy and convert it into electricity (photovoltaic) and heat (solar thermal.)

Spine Text

This study guide accompanies the living book *Wonders of Chemistry* by A. Frederick Collins. I highly recommend you purchase the newly reprinted Yesterday's Classics version rather than using the reprint by Forgotten Books as it is a print on demand from Archive.org and is missing several pages. You can still use that version if you have it, however, and I will note the page number for both versions in this guide.

- 249 pages, 20 chapters
- (76 pp, 6 chapters this term)
- Reading Level: grade 8-12
- Prerequisites: H.S. Chemistry (part 1)

Author Bio

Archie Frederick Collins (1869-1952) was a respected engineer, inventor, experimenter, and authority on wireless telegraphy. He wrote an incredible number of books and articles on topics including household mechanics, astronomy, chemistry, how-to manuals for piloting aircraft, submarines, rapid math, and more.
He wrote The Book of Stars to conform to the Tests of the Boy Scouts yet regarded it as a book that he hoped all would read. He thought all things in the sky, along with "the green grass, the trees, the birds and all other good things we have without price" should be looked at, enjoyed and valued to the fullest. In many of his books, A. Frederick Collins recommended that if the reader had any trouble or puzzles of understanding, they should write to him and he would gladly write back and do all he could to help. (Michele Jahncke)

Necessary Titles to Complement This Course

- *The Elements: A Visual Exploration of Every Known Atom in the Universe* by Theodore Gray (Black Dog & Leventhal, 2012, 240 pp.) You can purchase the book or an app for your iPad. Also, the book has been reproduced on Theodore Gray's website.
- *That's the Way the Cookie Crumbles* by Joe Schwarcz (ECW Press, 2002, 273 pp.) *Optional — only three chapters are assigned this term.

Schedule

This study guide includes 33 lessons, each requiring approximately 40 minutes. It can be scheduled in one of the following ways:

- Once a week for an entire year, allowing time for exams at the end of each term, and including other science subjects on the other days of the week, or
- Three times a week for 11 weeks allowing for exams during the 12th week.

Exams

You can download a digital copy of the exam questions for this study at https://qrs.ly/rzcnoev.

Broken Links & Errors

If you notice a broken link in this study guide, please email the author for a replacement: Nicole@SabbathMoodHomeschool.com. You can also view the Change Log at https://qrs.ly/1tfqkzm.

Science Notebook

Students should write narrations in their science notebook, including drawings, where appropriate, to better show what they have learned. This is not a test, so if they need to look at a diagram to copy it into their own book, that is acceptable. All reading, experiments, activities, and current events should be included, and each item should be dated. Students may also include quotes which they particularly liked from the reading. Learn more about keeping a science notebook in the SMH article, "Keeping a Science Notebook." (https://qrs.ly/racno3a).

Current Events

Each week, students should read a scientific current event. ScienceNewsforStudents.org is an excellent resource. Also, NewsELA, one of the best general news options for students, includes many scientific articles and allows you to change the difficulty of the text to your student's reading ability. You must create an account to view the articles on this site, but it is free and easy.

Other sites specific to chemistry news include:

- ChemMatters Magazine for High Schoolers
- Scientific American's chemistry news page
- American Chemical Society news page

Transcripts

The completion of parts 1, 2, and 3 counts towards one high school chemistry lab credit.

Leisure Reading Suggestions

Your students may like to read more about this science topic during their free time, so choose a few of the following books to purchase or check out from your local library.

- *Mendeleyev and His Periodic Table* by Robin McKown (191 pp.)
- *Doctor Paracelsus* by Sidney Rosen (214 pp.)
- *Uncle Tungsten: Memories of a Chemical Boyhood* by Oliver Sacks (352 pp.)
- *Robert Boyle: Founder of Modern Chemistry* by Harry Sootin (142 pp.)
- *The Chemist Who Lost His Head, The Story of Antoine Laurent Lavoisier* by Vivian Grey (112 pp.)
- *The Invention of Air* by Steven Johnson (276 pp.)
- *Antoine Lavoisier: Scientist and Citizen* by Sarah R. Riedman (192 pp.)
- *The Radium Woman* by Eleanor Doorly (196 pp.)
- *Napoleon's Buttons: How 17 Molecules Changed History* by Penny Le Couteur (390 pp.)
- *Oxygen: The Molecule that Made the World* by Nick Lane (384 pp.)
- *Mauve: How One Man Invented a Color that Changed the World* by Simon Garfield (240 pp.)
- *Molecules of Murder: Criminal Molecules and Classic Cases* by John Emsley (252 pp.)
- *The Chemy Called Al* by Wendy Isdell (154 pp.)
- *The Periodic Kingdom: A Journey into the Land of the Chemical Elements* by P. W. Atkins (161 pp.)
- Find more biographies on the chemistry page at SabbathMoodHomeschool.com.

Supply List

Gathering all necessary supplies in a box or plastic tub before beginning this course will benefit you greatly. When supplies are not on hand, experiments are often skipped.

Find a digital list and links to suggested products at www.SabbathMoodHomeschool.com/HSChem-supply-list.

Items marked with an asterisk (*) were used in part one.

HomeScienceTools.com or supply store

*Alcohol lamp and stand
*Denatured alcohol fuel
*pH paper
*Forceps or tongs
*Safety glasses
3 Beakers, 250 ml or small jars. One was purchased in part 1.
Stirring rod
Citric acid
Copper II (Cupric) Sulfate or Borax - sodium borate
Potassium Chloride or water softener salt
Sodium Carbonate
Lithium chloride
Inoculating needle, looped end or cotton swabs
Chewing Gum Kit
Multifiber test fabric strips
Sun Art paper
Untreated clover seeds
Rhizobium inoculum Note—The package should be kept in a cool place and out of direct sunlight
N-P-K Soil Test Kit

Hardware Store

Acetone (Find in the paint section of any hardware store.)
Clear acrylic sheet (comes with the paper) or a pane of glass from a frame
Flower pots or yogurt cups with holes in the bottom, 20 small
Saucers to put under the flower pots or a baking dish to set them all in
Seed-starting mix (Choose one with a low amount of nitrogen compounds.)
Nitrogen fertilizer
Grow light (optional, see Lesson 6)

Grocery Store

*Baking soda
*Food coloring (any color, optional, see Lesson 12 and 18)
*Lighter or matches
*Paper towel
*Rubber gloves, multiple sets, or a reusable pair
Permanent marker
Aluminum foil
Black construction paper
Borax
Box cutter or scissors
Chocolate bar
Clear packing tape
Clear plastic or glass plate or pie plate
Cornstarch
Glycerin
Graham crackers
Grease splatter screens for frying, 2. See image on Lesson 21
Large tub (approximately 1-gallon size)
Large, shallow container, such as a disposable aluminum roasting pan
Laundry detergent
Lemon Juice
Light corn syrup
Liquid starch
Marshmallows
Masking tape

Measuring spoons and cups (1 cup, ½ cup, 1 tablespoon, 1 teaspoon, ½ teaspoon)
Newspapers
Oven mitts
Parchment paper
Plastic wrap
Powdered Sugar
Red food coloring
Sponge
Strawberry flavoring
Strawberry Kool-Aid, 3 packages (or cherry, must include Red dye #40)
Thermometer
Toothpicks or tweezers
Vinegar
White glue
Ziplock bag, large freezer
Ziplock bags, small

Other

Cardboard pizza box

Around the House

Blender
Tap water, hot and regular
Clothes iron (optional, see Lesson 21)
Digital kitchen scale
Dry dish towel
Dried flower petals and leaves, finely chopped (optional, see Lesson 21)
Hair dryer (optional, see Lesson 21)
Interesting objects to print, such as a fern frond, leaves, flowers, or feathers.
Piece of cardboard
Plastic or metal spoon or a popsicle stick
Ruler, or a wooden spoon
Scissors or paper cutter
Scrap paper, 6-8 pieces
Sink with running water
Small bowls, 5

LESSON 1

Welcome back to high school chemistry. You will begin with the study of gunpowder! What does gunpowder, also known as black powder to distinguish it from modern gunpowder, have to do with chemistry? It is the earliest known chemical explosive, and who doesn't think of explosions when they think about chemistry.

Read: *Wonders of Chemistry.* Chapter 7 "From Gunpowder to TNT," pages 76-79. Place your bookmark at the title, "*How Smokeless Powders are Made.*" (Forgotten Books version, p. 85)

Please Note—Because you will be stopping part way through most of the chapters you read, I recommend that you find your stopping point, and move your bookmark to that location before you begin reading.

Notebook: After each reading, write all you have learned in your science notebook. Often questions will be included to prompt you, so you don't leave anything out. For example, 1) Tell the history of gunpowder. 2) How is gunpowder made? 3) What happens when gunpowder is fired?

Optional Activity: If you would like some inspiration for an artistic notebook page about the chemistry of gunpowder, take a look at Compound Interest's website. (https://qrs.ly/cacimfh)

Read: *The Elements*, Selenium, pp. 88-89.

Notebook: In your science notebook, make a drawing of your favorite representation of selenium and then write a short narration about this element.

LESSON 2

Today you will continue learning about chemical explosives.

Read: *Wonders of Chemistry.* Chapter 7 "From Gunpowder to TNT," pages 79-83. Place your bookmark at the title, *"About Detonators and What They Can Do."* (Forgotten Books version, p. 93)

Notebook: Write all you have learned from this reading in your science notebook. 1) Tell how smokeless gunpowder is made and how it is different from black powder. 2) Explain the composition of dynamite. 3) Tell how TNT is made.

Activity: If you are very interested in this subject, you may want to spend some of your free time watching the impressive video lecture, "Explosive Science" (https://qrs.ly/rscimjc, 1 hr.) by the Royal Institution. If you would rather not view the whole hour-long video, then just watch just the portions demonstrating: gunpowder (3:47-7:52 min.) and nitrocellulose (14:30-17:20 min.)

Read: *The Elements*, Bromine, pp. 90-91.

In your science notebook, make a drawing of your favorite representation of bromine and then write a short narration about this element.

LESSON 3—Experiment

Most people never have an opportunity to witness the effects of dynamite or TNT, but most have had a chance to hold a sparkler or watch a firework show. One of the key components in sparklers and firecrackers is black powder. Recall what you learned in Lesson 1 - what ingredients go into making black powder?

Black powder is used to propel aerial fireworks high into the sky, as well as cause the explosions necessary for special effects like noise or colored light. The colors are caused by different metal and salt compounds. Different metals burn in various colors. Today you will have an opportunity to test several metals to determine what color they would cause a firework to burn.

Activity: Metal flame test.

Supplies Needed—

- Rubber gloves
- Safety glasses
- Inoculating needle, looped end or use cotton swabs
- Alcohol lamp and stand
- Denatured alcohol fuel
- Lighter or matches
- 5 small bowls
- Lithium chloride
- Sodium Carbonate
- Copper II (Cupric) Sulfate (or use Borax - sodium borate, for the same color)
- Potassium Chloride (or use water softener salt)

Procedure—

Note: You must have an adult present and attentive while performing the following experiment. Some of the chemicals used can be hazardous if misused. All of them are at least an irritant, and many are toxic. Use caution when working with these chemicals. Read the information on the chemical label before you open each bottle and wear protective safety equipment, such as goggles and gloves.

1. Watch the video, "The Chemistry of Fireworks." (https://qrs.ly/nrcimjo, 6:31 min.)
2. Prepare a chart similar to the following in your science notebook:

Compound Name	Formula	Flame Color
Lithium chloride	LiCl	
Sodium Carbonate	Na_2CO_3	
Copper II (Cupric) Sulfate	$CuSO_4$	
Potassium Chloride	KCl	

3. Light your alcohol lamp.
4. Put on your safety glasses and gloves.
5. Wet the looped end of an inoculating needle in denatured alcohol. Hold it over the alcohol long enough to be sure it won't drip.
6. Pick up a small sample of one of the chemicals by dipping the loop into one of the chemicals.
7. Place the loop, with the chemical clinging to it, into the hottest portion of a flame from a burner.

8. Notice the color of the flame as the chemical sample burns. Record the color in your notebook.
9. Clean the wire by dipping the loop in denatured alcohol between samples.
10. Alternative Method—You can also demonstrate flame colors by making a small pile of one of the chemicals and wetting it with a few drops of flammable alcohol. Igniting the alcohol will burn the chemical and show its characteristic flame color.

If you need further explanation on how to conduct this experiment, you can watch the video, "Flame Test Lab." (https://qrs.ly/gpcipma, 8:28 min.) But keep in mind that you will spoil the surprise of seeing for yourself what color each metal creates.

Optional Activities:

1. If your family makes plans to have a bonfire, you may like to prepare some wax cakes containing chemicals to enjoy some "Colored Campfire Flames." (https://qrs.ly/zzcipn0.)

2. If you are working with a group, you might like to prepare some unknowns for the students to test. (https://qrs.ly/yucipn6)

Notebook: In your science notebook, record the name of each chemical and the color it produced. What did you learn from this experiment? Include drawings, if you would like.

Read: *The Elements*, Krypton, pp. 92-93.

Notebook: In your science notebook, make a drawing of your favorite representation of krypton and then write a short narration about this element.

LESSON 4

You have been reading about chemical explosives, primarily related to weaponry. You have also considered its use in fireworks. Can you think of some other uses for chemical explosions beyond these two applications?

Read: *Wonders of Chemistry.* Chapter 7 "From Gunpowder to TNT," pages 83-87. Place your bookmark on page 88. (Forgotten Books version, p. 98)

Notebook: Write all you have learned from this reading in your science notebook. 1) Tell what you know about detonators. 2) Tell about peacetime uses for dynamite.

Activity: Watch the video, "How Deadly Explosives Made the Nobel Peace Prize Possible" by Smithsonian (https://qrs.ly/18cipna, 7:03 min.)

Read: *The Elements*, Rubidium, pp. 94-95.

Notebook: In your science notebook, make a drawing of your favorite representation of rubidium and then write a short narration about this element.

LESSON 5

In today's lesson, you will start a new chapter of the text and begin learning how agriculture is affected by chemistry.

Read: *Wonders of Chemistry.* Chapter 8 "How Plants Live and Grow," pages 88-91. Place your bookmark on page 92 at the title, "*The Fixation of Nitrogen by Bacteria.*" (Forgotten Books version, p. 103)

Notebook: Write all you have learned from this reading in your science notebook. 1) Tell about the four kinds of land. 2) Explain how soil differs from other types of land. 3) Explain how land is kept fertile and how crop rotation is important to that end.

For Discussion: Have you read about the Dust Bowl? It was both a manmade and natural disaster. Man-made partly because the farmers did not implement crop rotation and other soil-conservation techniques. Farmers only planted high demand wheat crops, which depleted the land. Also, the wheat didn't anchor the topsoil the way the native prairie grass did, so the topsoil just blew away. Without topsoil, nothing could grow, and when a drought began in the early 1930s, the land was defenseless against the winds that buffeted the Plains.

Did you notice the date? All of this happened in the early 1930s, yet the value of crop rotation was described in your text, written in 1922. It was not until 1935 that farming techniques such as crop rotation were advocated by the government and farmers were even paid by the government to practice soil-conservation techniques.

Do you think this research was available to farmers at the time? Do you think there was a farmer's periodical, and do you think the farmers were capable of reading it? How important do you think it is for farmers to keep up with the modern research available?

Read: *The Elements*, Strontium, pp. 96-97.

Notebook: In your science notebook, make a drawing of your favorite representation of strontium and then write a short narration about this element.

LESSON 6—Experiment

Plants use nitrogen to make DNA in their cells and the proteins that lead to healthy stems and leaves. The problem is, although earth's atmosphere is made up of 78% nitrogen, this form of nitrogen, diatomic nitrogen, cannot be used by plants. They do not have the necessary enzyme, nitrogenase, to convert it into a form that they can use to make proteins. So how do plants get their nitrogen? Either through nitrogen deposits in the soil, such as added fertilizer, or by a friendly relationship with nitrogen-fixing bacteria. In this experiment, you'll compare which of those two methods results in the biggest clover patch.

Activity: Compare nitrogen-fixing bacteria to nitrogen fertilizers.

Supplies Needed—

- Untreated clover seeds
- Rhizobium inoculum
- N-P-K Soil Test Kit
- 2 small zipper bags
- Measuring spoon; ¼ tsp. Size
- Paper towels (2)
- Permanent marker
- Masking tape
- 20 small flower pots or yogurt cups with holes in the bottom
- Saucers to put under the pots or a baking dish to set them all in
- Seed-starting mix
- Plastic wrap
- Nitrogen fertilizer
- Digital kitchen scale
- Grow light (optional)

Procedure—

PART 1

1. Open the package of clover seeds and pour half of the package into each re-sealable plastic bag. Weigh each bag to be sure you have them as equal as possible.
2. Using the measuring spoon, add ¼ teaspoon of water to each plastic bag. (The water will help the rhizobium inoculum to stick to the clover seeds. Although you will not be adding rhizobia to both batches of seeds, you want to treat the seeds as similarly as possible, that is why you add water to both batches of seeds.)
3. Using a permanent marker, label one of the plastic bags: rhizobia coated.
4. Pour approximately 1.5 ounces of the Rhizobium inoculum into the plastic bag labeled rhizobia coated.
5. Seal both plastic bags and shake to thoroughly mix the water, clover seeds, and (in one of the two bags) the rhizobium inoculum.

6. Spread out two paper towels on a flat, dry surface, and pour each plastic bag of seeds onto its own paper towel. Label the paper towel with the rhizobia coated seeds.
7. Wait 30 minutes for the seeds to dry before proceeding to the planting part of the procedure.

PART 2

8. Put equal amounts of soil in each pot to about one inch from the top. Weigh each to be sure you have them as equal as possible.
9. Set the pots on saucers or in a pan and moisten each pot with equal amounts of water. You want the soil to be moist, but not soupy.
10. Using the masking tape and permanent marker, label the pots:
    a. 5 pots: no nitrogen added
    b. 5 pots: nitrogen fertilizer
    c. 5 pots: rhizobia
    d. 5 pots: rhizobia + nitrogen fertilizer
11. Plant seeds in each pot according to seed packet instructions.
12. In the pots labeled "no nitrogen added" and "nitrogen fertilizer" plant untreated clover seeds.
13. In the pots labeled "rhizobia" and "rhizobia + nitrogen fertilizer" plant the rhizobia coated clover seeds.
14. Cover the seeds with about half an inch of soil.
15. Sprinkle with water.
16. Cover with plastic wrap. (Plastic wrap over the containers creates the warmth needed for germination and holds in the moisture.)
17. Place the pots in a south-facing window. (If you don't have a bright south-facing window, then use a grow light. They should be exposed to this light 14 hours a day.)
18. Once the plants have germinated (emerged from the soil) remove the plastic covering.
19. Water the "no nitrogen added" and "rhizobia" pots with regular water. Water the "nitrogen fertilizer" pots with water and nitrogen fertilizer mixed according to the instructions on the fertilizer package. You may not need to add fertilizer at each watering.
20. The clover will grow to maturity in 5-6 weeks. When clover plants are mature, proceed with the experiment. (I will remind you.)

PART 3

Please Note—If you are doing three lessons per week, then you will complete this experiment during Lesson 24. If you are doing it once a week, then you will complete it during Lesson 12.

21. Use the soil test kit to measure the amount of nitrogen in the soil of each pot. Record the data in your lab notebook.
22. After these measurements are complete, carefully remove each plant from the soil and wash off any loose soil.
23. Blot the plants gently with a paper towel to remove any free surface moisture.
24. Weigh immediately (plants have a high composition of water, so waiting to weigh them may lead to some drying and therefore produce inaccurate data.)
25. Graph the average nitrogen levels in each category and the average biomass of the clover grown in each category. Which category had the highest levels of nitrogen? Which category produced the greatest biomass of clover? Was there any noticeable difference in the health or appearance of the clover grown with or without nitrogen fertilizer? Did inoculating the clover with rhizobia affect either the nitrogen levels in the soil or the total biomass?

This activity was adapted from Science Buddies: Bacteria Can Fix It!

Notebook: In your science notebook, record the steps you took to prepare this experiment. Include drawings, if you would like.

Read: *The Elements*, Yttrium, pp. 98-99.

Notebook: In your science notebook, make a drawing of your favorite representation of yttrium and then write a short narration about this element.

LESSON 7

Plants are complex chemical factories. They require raw materials, from which they make chemical compounds for their survival and defense. Today you will read about how plants get the materials they need.

Read: *Wonders of Chemistry.* Chapter 8 "How Plants Live and Grow," pages 91-96. Place your bookmark at the title, "*The Phosphate Fertilizers.*" (Forgotten Books version, p. 108)

Notebook: Write all you have learned from this reading in your science notebook. 1) How do clover, cowpeas, and the like give nitrogen back to the soil? 2) Tell about the various kinds of artificial fertilizers.

Current Event: Read the article, "Teen converts water pollutant into a plant fertilizer." (https://qrs.ly/pzcipo7, 2017) If you keep a separate notebook for current events, you can write your narration there.

Read: *The Elements*, Zirconium, pp. 100-101.

Notebook: In your science notebook, make a drawing of your favorite representation of zirconium and then write a short narration about this element.

LESSON 8

The three main macronutrients that plants require are Nitrogen (N) for leaf growth; Phosphorus (P) for the development of roots, flowers, seeds, fruit; and Potassium (K) for strong stem growth, movement of water in plants, promotion of flowering and fruiting. You have already learned how a plant gets nitrogen, and in today's reading, you will learn about the other two, phosphorus and potassium.

Read: *Wonders of Chemistry.* Chapter 8 "How Plants Live and Grow," pages 96-100. Complete this chapter. Place your bookmark on page 101. (Forgotten Books version, p. 114)

Notebook: Write all you have learned from this reading in your science notebook. 1) Tell what you know about phosphorus and the fertilizers made from it. 2) Tell what you know about potash.

For Discussion: The job description of an Agricultural Chemist is: "Help develop new chemicals to increase crop production and yield, defend against pests, and protect the environment." Do you think plants need our help? Is it right for humans to meddle in plant growth? Is there a point where we take our meddling too far?

Optional Activity: If you would like to learn more about genetic modification of agriculture, watch the movie, "Genetic Roulette the Gamble of Our Lives." (https://qrs.ly/vmcipon, 1 hour 24 min.)

Read: *The Elements*, Niobium, pp. 102-103.

Notebook: In your science notebook, make a drawing of your favorite representation of niobium and then write a short narration about this element.

LESSON 9

If you have gotten behind for some reason, this would be a good lesson to skip. If not, then you have the treat of reading *That's the Way the Cookie Crumbles* today.

Read: To learn more about Robert Boyle's discovery of phosphorus and its reaction with oxygen, read *That's the Way the Cookie Crumbles*, "From Alchemist to Scientist"; pages 237-240.

Notebook: Write all you have learned from this reading in your science notebook.

Read: *The Elements*, Molybdenum, pp. 104-105.

Notebook: In your science notebook, make a drawing of your favorite representation of molybdenum and then write a short narration about this element.

LESSON 10

Chemistry is a big part of your everyday life — in the foods you eat, the air you breathe, cleaning chemicals, your emotions, and every object you can see or touch. In the next chapter of the text, you will begin looking at the chemistry of everyday things, starting with a very yummy thing.

Sugar Cane Harvest

Read: *Wonders of Chemistry.* Chapter 9 "Chemistry of Every-Day Things," pages 101-105. Place your bookmark at the title, "*About Camphor.*" (Forgotten Books version, p. 118)

Notebook: Write all you have learned from this reading in your science notebook. 1) How does sugar cane get from a green plant in a field to white crystals on the table? 2) Reproduce the following image of a sucrose molecule.

Chemists now know that there are various types of sugar derived from different sources. The kind of sugar mentioned in this section, extracted and refined from either sugar cane or sugar beet, is *sucrose*. Sucrose is actually a chemical combination of two kinds of *simple sugars*, glucose, and fructose. When two sugar molecules are joined together, it is called a *disaccharide*.

Below is an image of the molecular structure of sucrose. It shows twelve carbon atoms, twenty-two hydrogen atoms and eleven oxygen atoms, ($C_{12}H_{22}O_{11}$) all combined in a very specific way. Can you believe that a single molecule of sucrose is so complex?

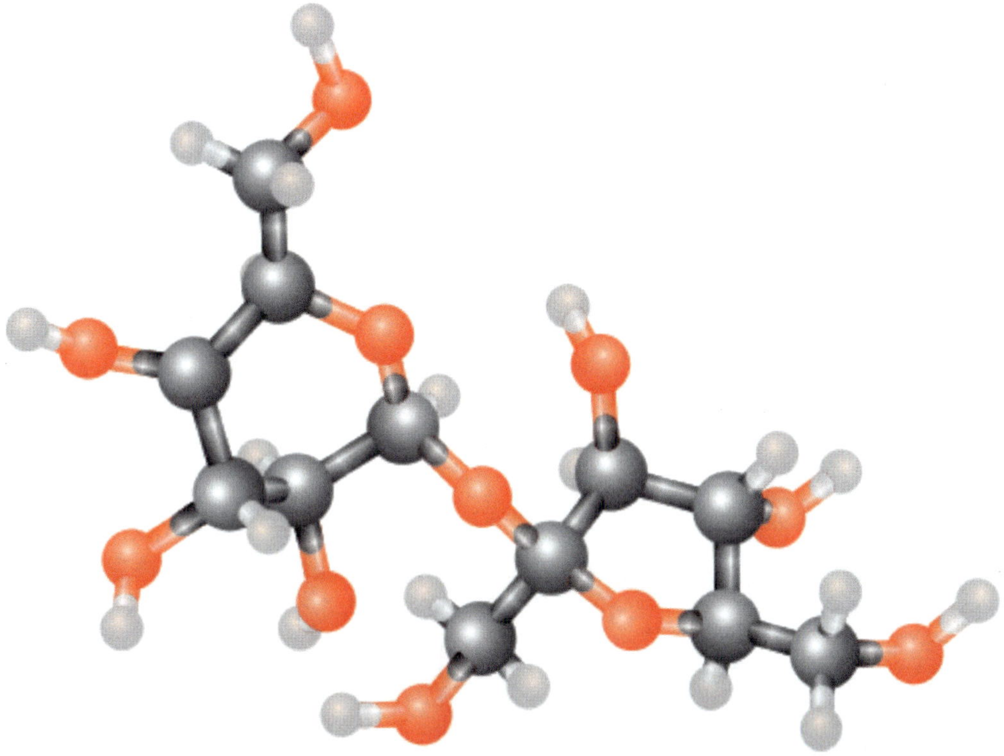

Source: William Crochot, [CC BY 4.0], via Wikimedia Commons

Current Event: To find a current article on this topic search Google for "sucrose" and then click the option for "News" at the top of the page. Read an article and write a narration of it. If you keep a separate notebook for current events, you can write your narration there.

Read: *The Elements*, Technetium, pp. 106-107.

Notebook: In your science notebook, make a drawing of your favorite representation of technetium and then write a short narration about this element.

LESSON 11

Have you ever smelled mothballs or Vicks Vapor Rub? The smell of both comes from the essential oil camphor, which you will learn about today.

Source: A Modern Herbal, [CC BY 2.0], via Botanical.com

Read: *Wonders of Chemistry.* Chapter 9 "Chemistry of Every-Day Things," pages 105-110. Place your bookmark at the title, *"About Rubber."* (Forgotten Books version, p. 123)

Notebook: Write what you have learned from this reading in your science notebook.

Essential oils have been used for thousands of years in various cultures for medicinal and health purposes. Their uses range from aromatherapy, household cleaning products, personal beauty care and natural medicine treatments. Camphor alone has been used in a wide variety of ways:

- An essential component in the production of smokeless gunpowder.
- One of the ingredients used by ancient Egyptians for mummification.
- To prevent rust in tool chests by releasing fumes that form a rust-preventative coating.
- An ingredient in sweets in ancient and medieval Europe.
- To treat sprains, swellings, and inflammation in ancient Sumatra.
- As a cough suppressant and as a decongestant today.

Other essential oils also offer a range of uses. An American favorite for headaches is a combination of peppermint and lavender essential oils daubed on the back of your neck. With your parent's permission, you may want to try it sometime. Learn about other uses of essential oils by reading the article, "101 Essential Oil Uses & Benefits" (https://qrs.ly/amcipov) by Dr. Axe.

Read: *The Elements*, Ruthenium, pp. 108-109.

Notebook: In your science notebook, make a drawing of your favorite representation of ruthenium and then write a short narration about this element.

LESSON 12—Experiment

Please Note—If you are working on this study guide once a week for an entire year, then it's time to complete the experiment you started in Lesson 6. If that is the case, save the following activity for Lesson 24 when everyone else will be completing the experiment begun in Lesson 6.

Activity: Cooking up chemical recipes.

Have you ever cooked dinner for your family? Did you follow a recipe or make it up as you went along? Chemical engineers have some things in common with chefs. Sometimes they follow a recipe to create the product they desire and other times they make up a recipe.

For example, a chemical engineer may receive a request for a particular item, maybe a plastic that can be used to make a child's doll. They may know just the right recipe to achieve the material requested or maybe they know of a recipe that will get them close, but they will still need to tweak the ingredients until they get the desired result.

Can you imagine having a "cookbook" of chemical concoctions on your bookshelf? Take a look at this one from 1896 called, "Chemical Recipes: Nearly One Thousand Modern Formulae for Producing All Kinds of Colors and Other Chemicals" by the Atlas Chemical Company. (https://qrs.ly/kmcipp7) You will find recipes for paints, soap, glue, putty, vinegar, baking powder, carbonated drinks, ink, and even baby food.

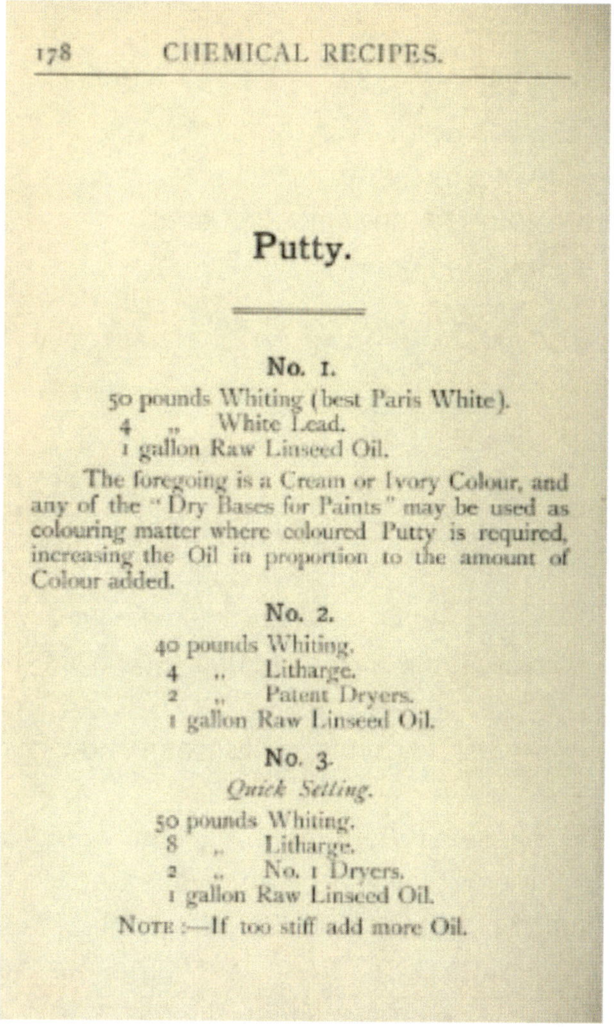
178 CHEMICAL RECIPES.

Putty.

No. 1.

50 pounds Whiting (best Paris White).
4 " White Lead.
1 gallon Raw Linseed Oil.

The foregoing is a Cream or Ivory Colour, and any of the "Dry Bases for Paints" may be used as colouring matter where coloured Putty is required, increasing the Oil in proportion to the amount of Colour added.

No. 2.

40 pounds Whiting.
4 " Litharge.
2 " Patent Dryers.
1 gallon Raw Linseed Oil.

No. 3.

Quick Setting.

50 pounds Whiting.
8 " Litharge.
2 " No. 1 Dryers.
1 gallon Raw Linseed Oil.

NOTE:—If too stiff add more Oil.

Source: *Chemical Recipes*, Atlas Chemical Company (Sunderland. 1896.) p 178

Would you like to create a material that could be used as a child's toy?

Supplies Needed—

- 1 ½ cup of water (divided)
- 2 tablespoons warm water
- ½ cup + 1 tablespoon white glue
- Food coloring (any color, optional)
- 1 ½ teaspoon of Borax (divided)
- 1 tablespoons cornstarch
- A sealed bag or container
- Something to stir with, such as a plastic or metal spoon or a popsicle stick
- Measuring spoons and cups
    - 1 cup
    - ½ cup
    - 1 tablespoon
    - 1 teaspoon
    - ½ teaspoon

Procedure—

Recipe for Slime
½ cup of water
½ cup of white glue
Food coloring (any color, optional)
1 teaspoon of Borax
1 cup of water

1. Combine 1/2 cup of water and 1/2 cup of white glue to make a glue mixture; **mix well**.
2. Add a few drops of food coloring to the mixture, if desired.
3. In a separate bowl, combine 1 teaspoon of Borax and 1 cup of water to make a Borax solution; mix until all of the borax is well dissolved.
4. Add the Borax solution to the glue mixture and stir.
5. Separate the congealed solid from the watery solution. Discard the watery solution.
6. Wash your hands with soap and water when you have finished the experiment.

If you have a little brother or sister, would the product of this recipe be a good thing for them to play with? Would you rather it oozes more? Then make it with less borax. Would you rather it be rubberier? Then make it with more borax. The amount of vigor you put into your stirring affects the final product as well. Did you add food coloring? What else could you add to the recipe to make it more fun for a child? Maybe some glitter or glow in the dark paint or substitute clear glue for the white glue.

Store your slime in a sealed baggie or container.

Recipe for a Bouncy Ball
2 tablespoons warm water
½ teaspoon Borax
Food coloring (any color, optional)
1 tablespoon of white glue
1 tablespoon of cornstarch

1. Combine 2 tablespoons of warm water and 1/2 teaspoon Borax to make a Borax solution; mix well.
2. Add a few drops of food coloring to the solution, if desired.
3. In a separate bowl, pour 1 tablespoon of white glue over 1 tablespoon of cornstarch. **Don't mix them yet.**
4. Add 1/2 teaspoon of the Borax solution to the cornstarch bowl. **Don't mix them yet.**
5. Let these ingredients sit for 10-15 seconds.
6. Begin stirring the mixture until it sticks together, then pick it up with your hands and roll it until you form a ball.
7. The more you play with the ball, the bouncier it will become.
8. Wash your hands with soap and water when you have finished the experiment.

Would the product of this recipe be a good thing for a child to play with? How would you change the recipe? You can try to adjust the amount of glue or cornstarch used to attempt to create a ball that makes a better toy.

Notebook: Write the recipes you used in your science notebook and report on how they worked out. Did you make any adjustments to the original recipe? If so, note them. Is there anything you would do differently next time? If so, note that also. Be sure to write neatly, because someone might want to follow your recipe someday. Maybe you have a little brother or sister, who would like to make more slime to play with or another bouncy ball.

Read: *The Elements*, Rhodium, pp. 110-111.

Notebook: In your science notebook, make a drawing of your favorite representation of rhodium and then write a short narration about this element.

LESSON 13

In the last lesson, you created a new material, a polymer, which is another name for plastic.

Polymerization is an important chemical process which produces many of the products found in our world today. Some polymer products that you may be familiar with include:

- Artificial fibers, such as nylon used in clothes and dacron used in soft drink bottles
- Synthetic rubber used in car tires
- Plastics, such as vinyl used in many medical products, polyethylene used in plastic bags, and PVC used in pipes
- Chewing gum
- Starch
- Wool
- Paint

To understand how polymerization works, imagine this scenario. You and your family attend a concert in the park. There are lots of people there, so to stay together, you hold hands as you move around. Sometimes your family slides right past another family that is moving around in the same way. Now suppose you see a family with whom you are friends. As you slide up next to each other, two other friends reach out and hold the arm of one member of each group to keep everyone together. Now the jostling crowd cannot separate you, and you can have a nice conversation.

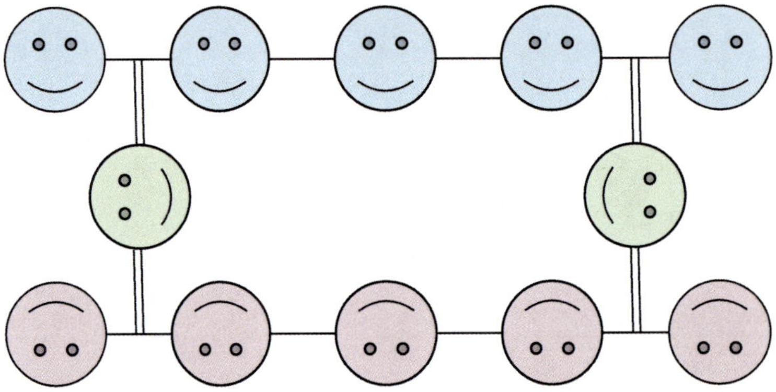

In this example, the individual members of your family represent small molecules called monomers. When you joined hands, you created a long chain of these molecules called a polymer. Lastly, the two other friends, who linked the two groups, represented crosslinkers. They held the two polymer chains together.

With that understanding, look at the monomer on the left below. It is a complete molecule. It is then repeated multiple times to create a polymer. This particular polymer is a glue similar to the white glue you used in your experiment. (PVA) These molecules easily slide past each other as a liquid.

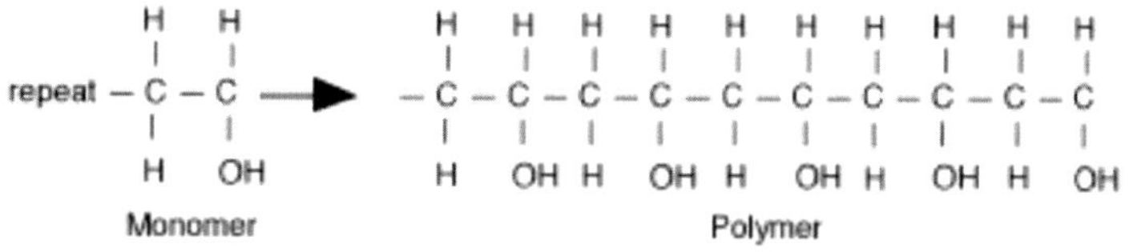

When Borax is mixed with water, it forms a borate ion, and when that solution is added to the glue solution, the borate ions link the long polymer molecules to each other so they cannot move as well. The borax crosslinks the polymer.

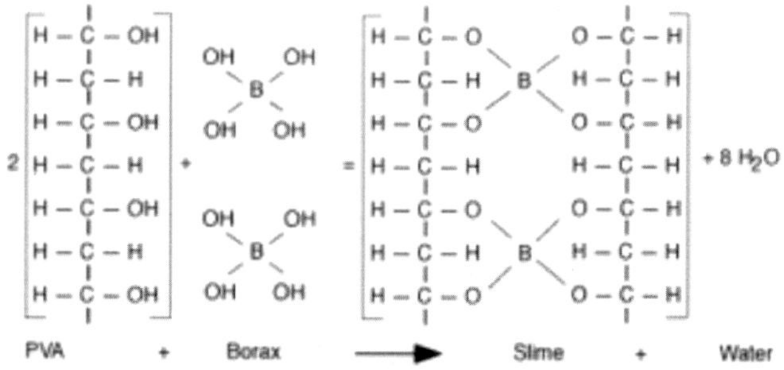

Notebook: Take a few minutes to write what you have learned about polymers. You may include drawings to help you explain what you know.

Read (if there is time): "The Basics: Polymer Definition and Properties" (https://qrs.ly/42cipph) by The American Chemistry Council. You may prefer to print this article so you do not have to read it on a screen.

Please Note—If you don't have enough time to read this entire article, scroll down to the header "Characteristics of Polymers."

Notebook: Write what you have learned about polymers from reading this article.

Read: *The Elements*, Palladium, pp. 112-113.

Notebook: In your science notebook, make a drawing of your favorite representation of palladium and then write a short narration about this element.

LESSON 14

In Lessons 12, you created a synthetic polymer. Today you will learn about a natural polymer — rubber. Natural rubber is an example of an *elastomer* type polymer. That means that the polymer molecule is coiled when in the resting state. The coils can double or triple in length when pulled and then snap all the way back when released.

Read: *Wonders of Chemistry.* Chapter 9 "Chemistry of Every-Day Things," pages 110-112. Complete this chapter. Place your bookmark on page 113. (Forgotten Books version, p. 128)

Notebook: Write all you have learned from this reading in your science notebook. 1) How is natural rubber harvested? 2) What are the benefits and drawbacks of rubber in its natural state? 3) Tell what is meant by the term vulcanization of rubber.

Trees that have been tapped to collect rubber.

Current Event: Read the article, "Songkhla builds six more rubber roads." (https://qrs.ly/bhcippt, 2017) If you keep a separate notebook for current events, you can write your narration there.

Afternoon nature walk: In the article, "Spider Silk Poised for Commercial Entry," Alex Scott said,

> "*Spider silk is by weight five times stronger than steel and three times tougher than Kevlar, a p-aramid fiber from DuPont. Strength is defined as the weight a material can bear, and toughness is the amount of kinetic energy it can absorb without breaking. The silk's primary structure is its amino acid sequence, mainly consisting of repeated glycine and alanine blocks.*
>
> *Potential applications include cables and bulletproof vests. Spider silk's antimicrobial properties make it suitable for wound patches. Because the silk is not rejected by the human body, it can be used to manufacture artificial tendons or to coat implants. And its thermal conductivity is similar to that of copper, but its mass density is one-seventh of copper's, making it a potential heat management material.*" [1]

When you take a nature walk this week, examine the mechanical properties of spider silk. Are the properties the same for the different types of silk produced by a single spider (dragline silk, sticky silk for trapping prey, silk used to support a web, etc.)? Is silk different from one type of spider to another? Does temperature affect the properties of the silk produced by a spider?

Read: *The Elements*, Silver, pp. 114-115.

Notebook: In your science notebook, make a drawing of your favorite representation of silver and then write a short narration about this element.

---

[1] Scott, Alex. "Spider Silk Poised for Commercial Entry." *Chemical and Engineering News*, American Chemical Society, 3 Mar. 2014, cen.acs.org/articles/92/i9/Spider-Silk-Poised-Commercial-Entry.html.

LESSON 15—Experiment

Have you ever chewed a piece of gum until all the sweetness was gone and you were left with just the gum base? That gum base is made of three things: a resin for chewiness, wax for softness, and elastomers that maintain its elasticity. Early chewing gum was from tree-based resins (such as natural rubber or chicle) and natural waxes (such as beeswax.) Today, however, most brands of gum use synthetically derived plastics for both of those ingredients.

The gum base you will use today is a completely plastic-free gum base:
Ingredients: natural rubber, calcium carbonate, hydrogenated soybean oil, soybean lecithin, vegetable oil, beeswax, and carnauba wax.

Activity: Make your own chewing gum.

Supplies Needed—

- Purchase a Chewing Gum Kit.
- Alternatively—
  - 1/3 cup gum base
  - 1/2 - 3/4 cup Powdered Sugar
  - 1/2 tablespoons light corn syrup
  - 1 teaspoon glycerin
  - 1/4 teaspoon citric acid
  - 6 drops of strawberry flavoring
  - 3 drops of red food coloring
  - Parchment paper cut into 3-inch squares

Procedure—

Please Note—If you purchased the kit, follow the directions that are included.

1. Put gum base, citric acid, corn syrup and glycerin in a bowl and microwave for 45 seconds.
2. Stir mixture and put back in for 5-10 seconds intervals until completely melted.
3. Add strawberry flavor and red food coloring and stir.
4. Set aside two tablespoons of powdered sugar to sprinkle over finished gum.
5. Sprinkle 1/4 cup powdered sugar on parchment paper.
6. Drop gum mixture on top of sugar and knead together. Continue kneading gum, mixing in remaining powdered sugar until gum is smooth and rollable; approximately 10 - 15 minutes.
7. Roll gum into a snake shape and cut into bite size pieces (about 1/2 inch.) Kitchen scissors work best.

8. Sprinkle each piece with powdered sugar and place in the middle of a parchment paper square; twisting each side to hold gum in place.

Gum bases for chewing gum are different from those for bubble gum. A bubble gum base is formulated with the ability to blow bubbles; it contains higher levels of elastomers or higher molecular weight polymers for this purpose. Gum bases for non-acid flavored gum use calcium carbonate as a filler, while gum bases for acid flavored gum use talc as a filler since acids can react with calcium carbonate to produce carbon dioxide gas, which is undesirable. Bubble gum usually contains 15-20% gum base, while chewing gum contains 20-25% gum base and sugar-free chewing gum contains 25-30% gum base.[2]

This activity was adapted from Dixie Crystals.

Optional Activities:

1. View an interactive slideshow showing the entire production process from extraction of the natural chicle through packaging of the finished gum on Glee Gum's website. (https://qrs.ly/7gcipqd.)

2. Read about the history of chewing gum on Serious Eats: "The History of Chewing Gum, From Chicle to Chiclets." (https://qrs.ly/j6cipr2.)

Read: *The Elements*, Cadmium, pp. 116-117.

Notebook: In your science notebook, make a drawing of your favorite representation of cadmium and then write a short narration about this element.

[2] "Gum Base." *Wikipedia*, Wikimedia Foundation, 30 July 2017, en.wikipedia.org/wiki/Gum_base.

LESSON 16

Today you will begin learning about fibers made from natural sources.

Read: *Wonders of Chemistry.* Chapter 10 "Cellulose and Other Fibers," pages 113-117. Place your bookmark at the title, "*Artificial Silks.*" (Forgotten Books version, p. 132)

Notebook: Write all you have learned from this reading in your science notebook.

Activity: If you have access to a microscope, look at the cellulose of a tree under it, as mentioned on page 130.

Read: *The Elements*, Indium, pp. 118-119.

Notebook: In your science notebook, make a drawing of your favorite representation of indium and then write a short narration about this element.

LESSON 17

As you continue this chapter on Cellulose and Other Fibers, you will learn how chemistry plays a part even in the natural fibers we use.

Vocabulary: **Inflammable:** easily set on fire, or flammable.

Read: *Wonders of Chemistry*. Chapter 10 "Cellulose and Other Fibers," pages 117-120. Place your bookmark at the title, "*Sheep and Wool Fibers.*" (Forgotten Books version, p. 137)

Notebook: Write all you have learned from this reading in your science notebook.

Activity: On page 133, you read, "The guncotton is now dissolved in ether and alcohol when collodion results." The next portion explains how a fiber is made, but if chemists stop there, they have a product, *collodion*, that can be used for other useful purposes. A flexible type of collodion can be applied to the skin to close small wounds, abrasions, and cuts, or to hold surgical dressings in place. Another, non-flexible kind of collodion is often used in theatrical make-up. When it is applied to the skin and allowed to dry, it shrinks, causing wrinkles and is therefore used to simulate old age, or scars.

If you would like to learn how collodion is used to simulate scarring, you can watch the video, "Rigid Collodion for Wounds and Scars." (https://qrs.ly/enciprg, 2:43 min.)

Read: *The Elements*, Tin, pp. 120-121.

Notebook: In your science notebook, make a drawing of your favorite representation of tin and then write a short narration about this element.

LESSON 18—Experiment

In Lesson 13 you learned that polymerization produces many of the products found in our world today, including artificial fibers, such as nylon. Nylon is the most common fiber for textiles. It is one of the strongest fabrics on the market. It can be easily dyed so fabrics can be made in a rainbow of colors. It is known to drape well. It is used in an almost countless number of items, such as backpacks, jackets, wedding gowns and bridal veils, athletic shoes, ponchos, umbrellas, camera cases, swimsuits, socks, gloves, hats, luggage, and much more.

You probably know that fabrics are made by weaving fibers together into different patterns. You may even have seen cotton or wool being spun, but have you considered how a synthetic fiber is pulled into long, continuous fiber?

The experiment you will perform today will demonstrate one way to make a fiber from a polymer. The industrial process is called cold drawing.

Activity: Making a plastic fiber.

Supplies Needed—

- Rubber gloves
- Safety glasses
- White glue
- Stirring rod
- Acetone
- Small jar or beaker
- Toothpicks or tweezers
- Sink with running water
- Paper towel

Procedure—

Please Note—Acetone is flammable and should not be used anywhere near a flame. As it evaporates readily, use it only in a well-ventilated room or outdoors, and keep its container tightly covered when not in use. Wear safety goggles and rubber gloves to protect your eyes and skin.

1. Put on your safety glasses and gloves.
2. Have your stirring rod close at hand.
3. Pour a little glue into a small jar to a height of about 1 cm (1/3 in.)
4. Dip one end of a toothpick into the glue and try to lift a strand out of it with the aid of the toothpick. You will find that the glue flows off the toothpick.
5. Tilt the jar a bit and carefully pour acetone down the inside of the jar to a height of about 1 cm (1/3 in.) The glue and acetone should be equal heights.
6. Lower the point of the toothpick into the jar until it is where the glue and acetone meet. (In other words, pass the toothpick through the acetone to where

the acetone and glue layers meet.) Alternatively, you can use a pair of tweezers for this step.

7. Gently lift a bit of the lower layer upward in the form of a fiber strand. It may take a little practice to get this to work, and you may have to pull out a clump to get it started.
8. When you have one end of an unbroken strand lifted above the jar, lay it over the stirring rod.
9. Carefully turn the rod to wind the fiber in a spiral around it. Keep the stirring rod only slightly above the jar, as the wet fiber is weak and will break if extended too far. With practice, you will find that you can wind the spiral along the entire length of the rod.
10. The fiber can be allowed to dry on the rod in a well-ventilated location.
11. When dry, you can unwind it from the rod.
12. Rinse the little jar thoroughly with water. Pour any used acetone into the sink and run water after it for about thirty seconds. Dry the jar with a paper towel.

The white glue used in this experiment is a solution of a hydrophilic polymer with a carbon backbone (polyvinyl acetate.) The glue also contains some water and other ingredients needed to improve its effectiveness.

Acetone was used because water is very soluble in it. The acetone dissolves the water in the polymer mix as the polymer is drawn from the solution, allowing the fiber to form.

Nylon fibers for fabrics and ropes are made by cold drawing in a process similar to the one in this experiment, although it is made by reacting two different monomers than you used.

Notebook: In your science notebook, record the steps you took and what you learned from this experiment. Include drawings, if you would like.

This activity was adapted from *Plastics and Polymers Science Fair Projects* by Madeline Goodstein.

Alternate activity: Make a natural plastic from dairy.

Plastics are generally produced from petroleum, but they can come from other sources as well. All that is really required is the ability to join molecules containing carbon and hydrogen together, which occurs when milk is curdled.

Supplies Needed—

- 1 C milk
- 4 Tsp vinegar or lemon juice
- Saucepan and stove, hot plate or other heat source OR a mug and a microwave
- Spoon
- Food coloring (optional)

Procedure—

1. Pour 1 cup milk in a saucepan and heat to a simmer over low to medium heat. (Alternatively, you can heat it in a microwave, but don't get it too hot.)
2. Remove from heat and stir in 4 teaspoons of white vinegar or lemon juice.
3. Stir until mixture with a spoon until it starts to gel and curds are formed.
4. Strain and rinse the curds with water. The curds are plastic!
5. Optional—Knead food coloring into your curds.
6. Form them into shapes, such as buttons or toys, and let them dry overnight.

The plastic is formed as a result of a chemical reaction between the casein in the dairy product and the acid (acetic in the vinegar, citric and ascorbic in the lemon juice.)

Notebook: In your science notebook, record the steps you took and what you learned from this experiment. Include drawings, if you would like.

This activity was adapted from ThoughtCo.: How to Make Natural Plastic from Dairy Products.

Read: *The Elements*, Antimony, pp. 122-123.

Notebook: In your science notebook, make a drawing of your favorite representation of antimony and then write a short narration about this element.

LESSON 19

Wool is the textile fiber obtained from sheep and other animals, including cashmere and mohair from goats, qiviut from muskoxen, and angora from rabbits. Wool has several qualities that distinguish it from hair or fur, mainly that it is crimped and elastic.

Read: *Wonders of Chemistry.* Chapter 10 "Cellulose and Other Fibers," pages 120-124. Place your bookmark at the title, "*Paper Making.*" (Forgotten Books version, p. 141)

Notebook: Write all you have learned from this reading in your science notebook. 1) Tell what you know about wool. 2) Tell what you know about silk.

Activity: If you have access to a microscope, look at wool under it, as mentioned on page 138.

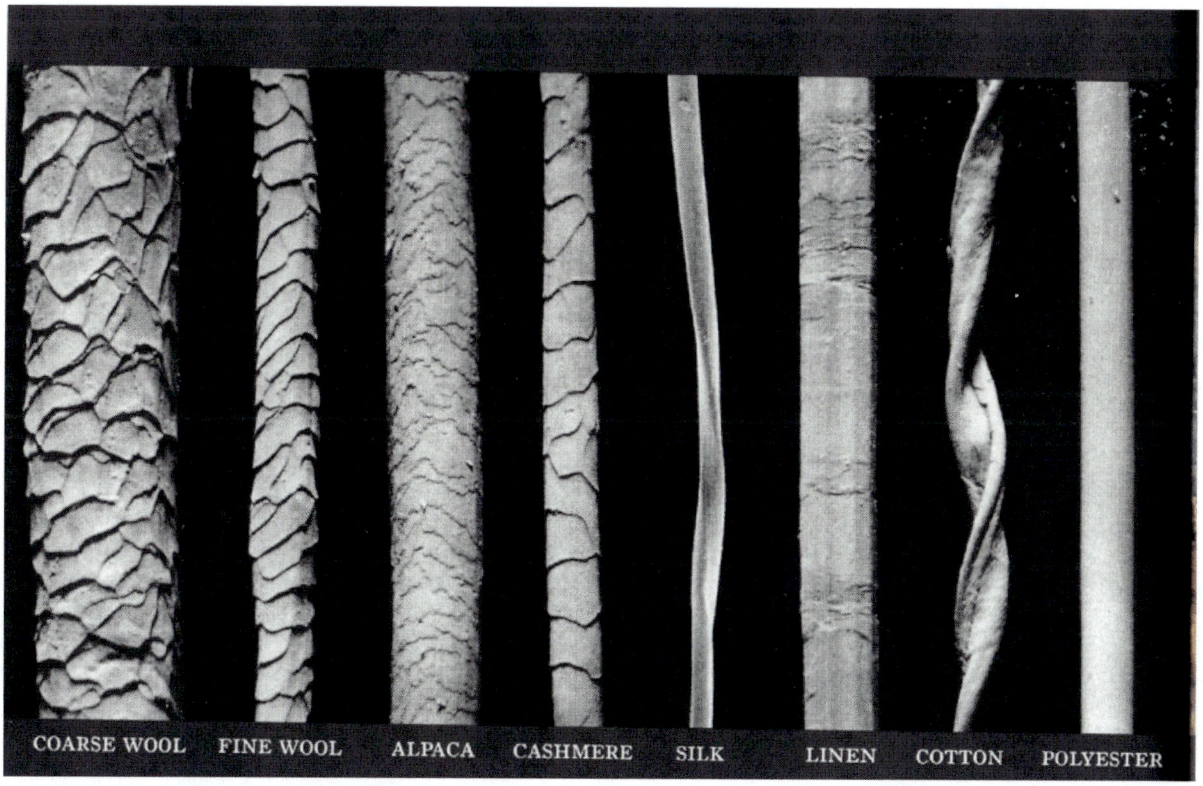

Read: *The Elements*, Tellurium, pp. 124-125.

Notebook: In your science notebook, make a drawing of your favorite representation of tellurium and then write a short narration about this element.

LESSON 20

The last fiber covered in this chapter is that of paper. Today you will learn how chemistry plays a part in the making of paper.

Read: *Wonders of Chemistry.* Chapter 10 "Cellulose and Other Fibers," pages 124-126. Complete this chapter. Place your bookmark on page 127. (Forgotten Books version, p. 144)

Notebook: Write all you have learned from this reading in your science notebook.

Activity: To view some of the machines used in papermaking, watch the video, "How Paper is Made?" (https://qrs.ly/ltciplx, 3:40 min.)

Read: *The Elements*, Iodine, pp. 126-127.

Notebook: In your science notebook, make a drawing of your favorite representation of iodine and then write a short narration about this element.

LESSON 21—Experiment

In the last lesson, you learned how paper is made on a large scale. Today you will learn to make handmade paper.

Activity: Make handmade paper.

Supplies Needed—

- 6-8 pieces of scrap paper
- Large, shallow container, such as a disposable aluminum roasting pan
- Blender
- Liquid starch
- 2 Grease splatter screens for frying, see image below
- Sponge
- Dry dish towel
- Water, hot and cool
- Scissors or paper cutter
- Hair dryer (optional)
- Finely chopped dry flower petals and leaves (optional)
- Clothes iron (optional)

Source: Jill Nystul, How to Make Beautiful Handmade Paper

Procedure—

1. Tear or cut the paper into 1-inch square pieces. No need to be precise here.
2. Put the paper in a blender and cover with hot tap water.
3. Let it sit for approximately 10 minutes.
4. Pulse the paper/water mixture in your blender a few times until you get a slurry.
5. Fill the large, shallow container with a couple of inches of water.
6. Then add your paper slurry to the water and mix it up.

7. Stir 2 teaspoons of liquid starch into the pulp mix. The starch helps prevent ink from soaking into the paper fibers.
8. Optional—You can add finely chopped dried flower petals and leaves to your slurry if you would like.
9. Submerge one of your screen splatter guards in the slurry mixture.
10. Then slowly bring it up out of the mix, holding it as level as you can, until it is evenly covered. You might need to try this a couple of times to get nice, even coverage.
11. Keep it over the container until most of the water has drained from the pulp.
12. Place the screen with the wet paper mixture onto a dry dish towel and cover it with the other screen splatter guard.
13. Using a sponge, pat the screen all over to soak up as much excess water as possible. Squeeze the excess water from the sponge back into the container with the slurry mixture. Continue until you have most of the water out.
14. Remove the top screen and gently lift the paper from the screen. If it sticks to the screen, you may have pulled too fast or not pressed out enough water.
15. You can speed up the drying process by using a hair dryer on the low setting, but it won't dry as flat.
16. Optional—Use an iron set on high to dry the paper quickly and give it a bit of shine.
17. Cut your paper into whatever shape you would like. For example, you might cut it and fold it into small greeting cards.
18. Test your pen on a scrap piece of your homemade paper to be sure it won't bleed when you write on it.

If you would like to make more paper in the future, you might like to follow the instructions, "Make a Mould and Deckle for Handmade Paper." (https://qrs.ly/k9ciplk.)

This activity was adapted from Jill Nystul's Blog: OneGoodThing.com.

Read: *The Elements*, Xenon, pp. 128-129.

Notebook: In your science notebook, make a drawing of your favorite representation of xenon and then write a short narration about this element.

LESSON 22

Today, if you go outside to create a painting of a flower for your nature study notebook, you likely only need to open your case of watercolor paints to get started, but that convenience has only been an option for the last couple hundred years.

"Most Renaissance or Baroque painters worked for several years as an apprentice in the workshop of a master artist, where they studied the skills of drawing, painting, and also how to make and mix paint. Knowledge of colour pigments, their properties (hue, permanence, chroma, lightfastness, compatibility with other pigments, drying attributes), and how to make them into oil paint was an essential part of every painter's art training. Even the grinding of a pigment required skill as the particle-size needed to be fine and regular, and a small number of pigments can be damaged by incorrect grinding. In addition, it was important to know the correct binder-to-pigment proportions (which may vary from 10 percent or less, to as high as 150 percent), and also whether or not a particular pigment requires the addition of a siccative or extender before being ready for use."[3]

Read: *Wonders of Chemistry.* Chapter 11 "Colors, Pigments and Plants," pages 127-130. Place your bookmark at the title, "*Natural Pigments.*" (Forgotten Books version, p. 148)

Please Note—If your copy of the text is missing pages 144, 145, and 147, you can get them here: https://qrs.ly/ngcipkk.

Notebook: Write all you have learned from this reading in your science notebook. 1) Tell the uses and history of paint. 2) Tell what you know about watercolors and oil paints.

For Discussion: If the paint of the masters had to be mixed on a daily basis, can you imagine the difficulties artists might have had when painting a huge canvas that took years to complete? Do you think you might be able to notice some variation in paint color or consistency if you know to look for it?

Optional Activity: To learn more about how art, chemistry, and technology have interacted throughout the ages read the book *Bright Earth: Art and the Invention of Color* by Philip Ball.

Read: *The Elements,* Cesium, pp. 130-131.

Notebook: In your science notebook, make a drawing of your favorite representation of cesium and then write a short narration about this element.

---

[3] "Oil Painting." *Oil Painting: History, Famous Paintings in Oils,* www.visual-arts-cork.com/oil-painting.htm.

LESSON 23

Today you will learn about natural and chemical pigments.

Natural Iron Oxides Dry Pigments: Yellow Ochre, Raw Sienna, Burnt Sienna, Raw Umber, and Burnt Umber

Read: *Wonders of Chemistry.* Chapter 11 "Colors, Pigments and Plants," pages 130-135. Place your bookmark at the title, "*How Lakes are Made.*" (Forgotten Books version, p. 153)

Notebook: Write all you have learned from this reading in your science notebook.

For Discussion: The use of white lead paint, (mentioned on page 149-150,) peaked in 1922, the year this book was written. This paint was much sought-after because it was washable and durable. Shortly after that, chemists working for paint manufacturers began developing new formulas for paints. Casein (milk protein) was mixed with formaldehyde, ammonia, or borax, to create many different types of paints. In 1935, a new water-based casein paint was developed with the use of synthetic rubber and styrene. This recipe was the first latex paint and gained great commercial success.

However, American consumers started to become aware that many of these paint formulas posed health risks as the lead and mercury in the paint were highly toxic. In 1978, the federal government banned consumer uses of lead paint, and in 1990 the use of mercury in interior latex paint was banned.

Read: *The Elements*, Barium, pp. 132-133.

Notebook: In your science notebook, make a drawing of your favorite representation of barium and then write a short narration about this element.

LESSON 24—Experiment

Please Note—If you are working on this study guide three times a week for one term, then it's time to complete the experiment you started in Lesson 6. If you are working on this study guide once a week for an entire year, then you can complete the activity from Lesson 12 today.

Notebook: In your science notebook, record the steps you took and what you learned from this experiment. Include drawings, if you would like.

Read: *The Elements*, Lanthanum, pp. 134-135.

Notebook: In your science notebook, make a drawing of your favorite representation of lanthanum and then write a short narration about this element.

LESSON 25

Vocabulary: **Lake:** A purplish red pigment prepared from lac or cochineal.

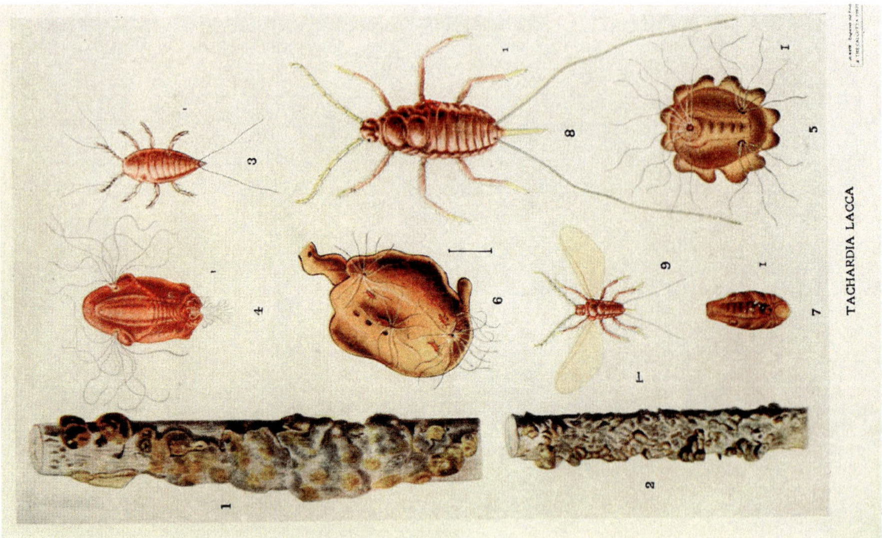

Kerria lacca, a species of insect in the family Kerriidae, the lac insects.

Source: *Indian Insect Life: a Manual of the Insects of the Plains* by Harold Maxwell-Lefroy

Read: *Wonders of Chemistry.* Chapter 11 "Colors, Pigments and Plants," pages 135-138. Complete this chapter. Place your bookmark on page 139. (Forgotten Books version, p. 157)

Notebook: Write all you have learned from this reading in your science notebook.

Activity: In a detail of the painting *The Vendramin Family Venerating a Relic of the True Cross*, Titian used glazes of red lake to create the vivid crimson of the robes. The red lakes were particularly important in the history of art, allowing the artist to achieve a vibrant, rich red color. They were often used to depict elegant draperies and fabrics.

Carmine lake was originally produced from the cochineal insect, native to Central and South America. It is also called crimson lake. When the Spanish conquered the Aztec Empire (1518-1521), they encountered Aztec warriors garbed in an unknown crimson color. Cochineal became their second most valuable export from the New World, after silver, and the Spanish zealously guarded the secret of its production for centuries. Today the bright-red synthetic pigment carmine has taken its place. It is obtained from the aluminum salt of carminic acid.[4]

[4] "Lake Pigment." *Wikipedia*, Wikimedia Foundation, 1 July 2017, en.wikipedia.org/wiki/Lake_pigment.

Take a few minutes to appreciate the rich color Titian used in the picture below, and if you ever have the opportunity to visit an art museum with 16th-century art on display, be sure to spend some time admiring the work of the artist and the ancient chemists.

Source: Titian, [Public Domain], via Wikimedia Commons

Read: *The Elements*, Cerium, pp. 136-137.

Notebook: In your science notebook, make a drawing of your favorite representation of cerium and then write a short narration about this element.

LESSON 26

In Lesson 23 you learned about chemical pigments. Today you will learn about the discovery of *mauveine*, the first chemically-produced dye.

Vocabulary: **Coal tar:** A thick, black, viscid liquid formed during the distillation of coal.

Read: *That's the Way the Cookie Crumbles*, "Mauving On"; pages 222-226.

A postage stamp using mauve dye.

Notebook: Write a narration of this chapter in your science notebook.

Optional Activity: If you would like to learn more about the history of William Henry Perkin, read the book *Mauve: How One Man Invented a Color that Changed the World* by Simon Garfield.

"Mauve fell out of fashion in the late 1860s, overtaken by the burgeoning palette of the synthetic dye industry, but not before Perkins made his fortune and birthed synthetic chemistry as a business."[5]

-PENNY. "KINGY GRAPHIC DESIGN HISTORY."

Read: *The Elements*, Praseodymium, pp. 138-139.

Notebook: In your science notebook, make a drawing of your favorite representation of praseodymium and then write a short narration about this element.

---

[5] Penny. "Kingy Graphic Design History." *PENNY: Post 1: Swooning Mauve*, 1 Jan. 1970, kingygraphicdesignhistory.blogspot.com/2010/05/penny-post-1-swooning-mauve.html.

LESSON 27—Experiment

The modern dye industry started 150 years ago with the discovery of "mauve," the first synthetic dye. Since then, thousands of dyes have been developed to work with all types of fabrics. However, the affinity of a dye for a kind of fabric depends on the chemical structure of the dye and fabric molecules and the interactions between them.

Activity: Experiment with dyeing various fibers.

Supplies Needed—

- Rubber gloves
- 3 multifiber test fabric strips (This fabric contains strips of wool, acrylic, polyester, nylon, cotton, and acetate, in the order shown to the right.)
- 3 medium jars or beakers
- 3 packages of strawberry Kool-Aid (or cherry, must include Red dye #40)
- Vinegar
- Baking soda
- Water
- pH paper
- Stirring rod or popsicle stick
- Forceps or tongs
- Large tub (approximately 1-gallon size)
- Laundry detergent
- Permanent marker
- Paper towels

Procedure—

Please Note—Red dye #40, present in strawberry Kool-Aid, is a strong stain and will stain your skin and clothing.

1. Put on your gloves.
2. Label the first jar #1, and fill it half full with cool water.
3. Label the second jar #2, and fill it half full with vinegar.
4. Label the first jar #3, and fill it half full with hot vinegar.
5. Add 1 tsp of strawberry Kool-Aid to each jar and stir to combine.
6. The Kool-Aid includes citric acid, so it will cause the pH in each jar to be slightly acidic. (Approximately pH 2)
7. To neutralize the citric acid in the first beaker, slowly add baking soda. Carbon dioxide will be created at first, so add the baking soda slowly or the water will overflow. Continue to add baking soda a little at a time until the foaming stops, and then add more until it is approximately a pH of 8.
8. Label your multifiber test fabric pieces with #1, #2, and #3, then add the appropriate piece to each jar, pushing it down with the stirring rod.
9. Let it sit for at least one minute.

10. In the meantime, fill a large tub with water and 1-tablespoon of laundry detergent. Stir to combine.
11. One at a time, use forceps to remove the fabric pieces from the jars, rinse them well in the soapy water solution. Swish the fiber or rub it in your hand to remove any dye that has not adhered to the fabric. Squeeze the fabric to remove excess water, and lay in on a piece of paper towel.
12. Compare the results. Which fabric(s) consistently developed the most intense color, regardless of the type of dye used? Which fabric was the most difficult to dye? Which color solution created the best results?
13. You may allow the fabrics to dry overnight to see if there is any difference once they have dried.

Wool
Acrylic
Polyester
Nylon
Cotton
Acetate

Chemical bonds play a significant role in how and why dyes work. Cotton, wool, and silk are natural fibers obtained from plants and animals, and acrylic, polyester, rayon, and nylon are synthetic fibers made from petrochemicals. Acetate, also called cellulose acetate, is prepared by chemical modification of natural cellulose. All fabrics, both natural and synthetic, are polymers, long chain molecules made up of multiple repeating units of small molecules. Some of these chains have several binding sites for dye molecules, and some have few binding sites. Looking at your results, which fabrics have the most binding sites and which the least?

Optional Extension: This activity was adapted from ChemEd XChange: "Kool-aid, Cotton, and Intermolecular Forces." (https://qrs.ly/aecipjy.) By visiting their site, you can view a short lecture from Tom Kuntzleman Spring Arbor University, Professor of Chemistry, explaining the extent of dyeing observed when all eight fibers are treated with the red dye #40. He sets up the experiment in the first four minutes and then his explanation is from 4:25 min to 20:33 min.

For Discussion: The ingredients in strawberry Kool-Aid are citric acid, salt, red #40, calcium phosphate, ascorbic acid, natural & artificial flavor. Do you think any of the ingredients affect the results? What kind of experiment could you set up to test your theory? Are there any other questions you have that could be answered through further testing?

Notebook: In your science notebook, record the steps you took and what you learned from this experiment. Include drawings, if you would like. You may also dry your test fabrics and tape or glue them into your notebook.

Optional Activities:

1. If you would like to learn more about the chemistry of food colorings, read the article, "Eating with Your Eyes" (https://qrs.ly/a8cipk5) by Brian Rohrig.

2. Watch the video, "Learn How to Hand Paint Yarn with Kool-Aid" (https://qrs.ly/5fcipkd, 5:10 min.) by naztazia.com.

Read: *The Elements*, Neodymium, pp. 140-141.

Notebook: In your science notebook, make a drawing of your favorite representation of neodymium and then write a short narration about this element.

LESSON 28

We often think of chemistry as the work of people mixing chemicals. However, chemistry happens in the world around you every day. One of the most common everyday chemical reactions and also one of the most remarkable is when plants chemically combine water from the soil and carbon dioxide from the air to produce glucose and oxygen. Today you will learn how the sun provides the energy needed for that chemical reaction.

Read: *Wonders of Chemistry.* Chapter 12 "The Wonders of Air," pages 139-143. Place your bookmark at the title, "*How Light Acts on Chemicals.*" (Forgotten Books version, p. 161)

Notebook: Write all you have learned from this reading in your science notebook.

Activity: Today you learned that the sun provides the energy needed for the chemical reaction photosynthesis. Have you ever wondered if there is a similar chemical reaction that takes place in humans? One dermatologist explains why he thinks so. To learn more, watch the TedTalk video, "Could the sun be good for your heart?" (https://qrs.ly/52cipjj, 12:10 min.)

Read: *The Elements*, Promethium, pp. 142-143.

Notebook: In your science notebook, make a drawing of your favorite representation of promethium and then write a short narration about this element.

LESSON 29

In the last lesson, you learned how the sun's rays provide the energy for chemical reactions in plants. Today you will read about the chemical reaction that happens when the sun's rays fall on various silver compounds and the way people have utilized that reaction throughout history.

Silver nitrate, $AgNO_3$

Source: W. Oelen, [CC BY 3.0], via Wikimedia Commons

Read: *Wonders of Chemistry.* Chapter 12 "The Wonders of Air," pages 143-148. Place your bookmark at the title, "*The Modern Dry Plate Process.*" (Forgotten Books version, p. 168)

Notebook: Write all you have learned from this reading in your science notebook. 1) How does light affect silver compounds? 2) How does light facilitate the creation of photographs?

Read: *The Elements*, Samarium, pp. 144-145.

Notebook: In your science notebook, make a drawing of your favorite representation of samarium and then write a short narration about this element.

LESSON 30—Experiment

You read that plants capture the sun's energy through photosynthesis. Humans have also found ways to capture the sun's energy and convert it into either electricity (photovoltaic) or heat (solar thermal.) The first experiment below tests the capture of thermal energy. The second experiment tests the conversion of solar energy into electricity using a solar cell. You can choose to do whichever experiment interests you the most.

Activity: Build a solar oven.

Supplies Needed—

- Cardboard pizza box (the kind delivered pizza comes in)
- Box cutter or scissors
- Aluminum foil
- Clear packing tape
- Plastic wrap or a large freezer zipper bag
- Black construction paper
- Newspapers
- Ruler, or a wooden spoon
- Clear plastic or glass plate or pie plate
- Thermometer
- Chocolate bar
- Marshmallows
- Graham crackers
- Oven mitts

Procedure—

1. Use a box knife or sharp scissors to cut a flap in the lid of the pizza box. Cut along three sides — front, left, and right — about an inch from the edges of the lid. If you plan to use a zipper bag to cover the opening you are creating, then be sure to cut the flap a bit smaller than the bag.
2. Fold this flap out so that it stands up when the box lid is closed.
3. Cover the bottom (inner) side of the flap with aluminum foil by tightly wrapping foil around the flap, then taping it to the top (outer) side of the flap. This will reflect the rays of the sun.
4. Open the box and tape a double layer of plastic wrap or a single layer of zipper freezer bag over the opening you made when you cut the flap in the lid. Tape around it entirely to create an airtight window for sunlight to enter into the box.
5. Line the bottom of the box with black construction paper that will absorb heat. The black surface is where your food will be set to cook.
6. To insulate the solar oven, so it holds in more heat, line the edges of your box with rolled up sheets of newspaper. It may be helpful to tape the rolls first, so they don't unroll, and then tape them down so that they form a border around

the cooking area. Be sure the newspaper rolls do not prevent your lid from closing.

7. Place a thermometer inside your oven so that you can check the temperature.
8. Put whatever food you will be cooking onto a clear plastic or glass plate or pie plate to prevent the bottom of your oven from getting dirty.
9. To make s'mores, place chocolate and marshmallows between two graham crackers. Place the s'mores inside the box and close the lid of the box.
10. Take your solar oven outside when the sun is high overhead (preferably between 11 am and 3 pm.) Set it in a sunny spot and position it so that sunlight is reflected from the foil covered flap into the plastic-covered window. Use a ruler to prop the flap at the right angle. You may want to angle the entire box by using a rolled-up towel.
11. Check your oven every 15 minutes to see if your s'mores are ready to eat.
12. When your food is through cooking, open the lid of the pizza box, and use oven mitts to lift the glass dish out of the oven.

Source: Gerry Dincher, [CC BY 2.0], via Flickr

Solar ovens come in many shapes and sizes. You may like to experiment with different types of boxes or bowls to see which design cooks food the fastest.

This activity was adapted from HomeScienceTools.com: Build a Solar Oven.

Alternate or Optional Activity: Experiments with photovoltaic cells

Supplies Needed—

- Three 0.5-volt PV cells, at least 10 square centimeters (1.5 sq. in) in size each, (found at most science supply companies and electronic stores)
- Several sheets of colored transparency film in various colors, including yellow and blue (office supply stores) Small pieces should be cut beforehand just to cover the PV cells.
- 30 cm of thin electrical wire (use with alligator clips unless the meter leads have alligator clips on their ends)
- DC ammeter (reads amps)
- DC voltmeter
- Direct sunlight (desk lamp or flashlight could be substituted)
- Aluminum foil
- Protractor
- Goggles
- Hair dryer

Procedure—

1. Open the instructions from the University of Oregon and print pages 7-12. (https://qrs.ly/wjcipis)
2. Complete the experiment as instructed.

Notebook: In your science notebook, record the steps you took and what you learned from the experiment(s) you completed. Include drawings, if you would like.

Read: *The Elements*, Europium, pp. 146-147.

Notebook: In your science notebook, make a drawing of your favorite representation of europium and then write a short narration about this element.

LESSON 31

"In our present state of knowledge, it cannot be done," stated 19th-century chemist Jean Dumas, when asked to comment on production of permanent pictures from images produced by a lens, "but I cannot say it will always remain impossible, nor set the man down as mad who seeks to do it."[6]

-MATTHEW DESOUZA

Read: *Wonders of Chemistry.* Chapter 12 "The Wonders of Air," pages 148-151. Complete this chapter. (Forgotten Books version, p. 171)

Notebook: Write all you have learned from this reading in your science notebook. 1) How did the dry plate process differ from the wet plate process you read about last time? 2) What do you know about color photography?

Read: *The Elements*, Gadolinium, pp. 148-149.

Notebook: In your science notebook, make a drawing of your favorite representation of gadolinium and then write a short narration about this element.

---

[6] DeSouza, Matthew. "A Winning Essay." *Chemistry Hall of Fame*, www.chem.yorku.ca/hall_of_fame/essays00/AgNO3.htm.

LESSON 32

You have completed the pages assigned in this term, so today you have some options.

Option #1: If you would like to learn how a camera works, watch the video, "How Does a Camera Work?" (https://qrs.ly/xjcimk1, 14:43 min.). This lecture explains the progression of the camera from a basic pinhole-camera into a modern digital camera.

Option #2: Read one or more of the following sections from *That's the Way the Cookie Crumbles*:

- "A Run on Stockings"; pages 183-186
- "A Rubber Match"; pages 186-190
- "Oobleck and Beyond"; pages 190-193

Option #3: If you have gotten behind for some reason, you can just skip this lesson.

Notebook: Write a narration in your science notebook.

Read: *The Elements*, Terbium, pp. 150-151.

Notebook: In your science notebook, make a drawing of your favorite representation of terbium and then write a short narration about this element.

LESSON 33—Experiment

"Have you ever seen a blue photograph? If you lived in the 1800s you would have. By placing objects on special paper and exposing the paper to sunlight, early photographers created blue images, called cyanotypes or sun prints. The process was also used for copying architectural plans called blueprints. Architects drew their plans in ink on very thin paper, then placed the drawings against blueprint paper and left them in the sun. The light was blocked in the places that had ink but passed through where there was no ink. When the blueprint paper was washed in clear water, the plans appeared as white lines on blue paper."

-THE J. PAUL GETTY MUSEUM [7]

Activity: Make a cyanotype.

Supplies Needed

- Sun Art paper
- Clear acrylic sheet or a pane of glass from a frame
- Pan large enough to lay a sheet of paper in
- Water
- Lemon juice (if the paper you purchased requires it)
- Interesting objects to print, such as a fern frond, leaves, flowers, or feathers.
- Paper towel or piece of cardboard

Procedure–

- Add water to the pan. Add a few drops of lemon juice to the water if the paper you purchased instructs you to add it.
- Because the blue molecules embedded in the paper are sensitive to ultraviolet light, it is best to prepare your print in a place where the sun's light cannot reach the paper as you arrange objects on top of it. Direct sunlight will expose the paper quickly, but even ambient light in the shade, or in a room with a big window will cause slow exposure of the paper.
- Arrange your objects on a piece of sun art paper.
- Place the clear acrylic sheet on top to flatten and hold your items to the paper.
- Take your paper and arrangement outside and lay it in direct sunlight for 3-5 minutes, or until it turns a very light blue or white. If no direct sunlight is

---

[7] "Sun Prints: Cameraless Photographs." *Sun Prints: Cameraless Photographs (Education at the Getty)*, www.getty.edu/education/kids_families/do_at_home/artscoops/sun_prints.html.

available, don't worry — just expose your print a little longer and wait for the same fading effect. Under cloud cover, the process may take 5-20 minutes.
- Rinse your paper in a pan of water for 1-5 minutes (as instructed for the paper you use.) The white will turn blue and the blue will turn white.
- Lay your paper flat on a paper towel or piece of cardboard to dry.

What has happened?

When set in the sun, two molecules present in the paper interact to form a new molecule. This chemical reaction is initiated by specific wavelengths of ultraviolet light. Because the blue molecules are converted into a new molecule that is colorless, the white of the paper base begins to show through. Areas of the paper that are blocked from the sun's rays still contain the original molecules, so they remain blue.

When the paper is placed in water two things happen: 1) Because the original blue compound is water soluble, it is washed away, leaving only the white paper base showing. The colorless compound created when you placed the paper in the sun is not water soluble, however, so it is not washed away, 2) Just as sunlight stimulated a chemical change in the previous step, the water stimulates another chemical change in this one. The water causes an oxidation reaction that turns the colorless compound into a deep blue color.

When you take your paper out of the water, the active chemical will not have finished oxidizing, but the water remaining in the paper will finish the job before it evaporates. By the time it is all gone you will have a beautiful, deep blue print.

Image source: Whit Andrews, [CC BY 2.0], via Flickr
This activity was adapted from SunPrints.org: How it Works.

Notebook: In your science notebook, record the steps you took and what you learned about sun prints. Possibly include your sun print in your notebook once it is dry.

Read: *The Elements*, Dysprosium, pp. 152-153.

Notebook: In your science notebook, make a drawing of your favorite representation of dysprosium and then write a short narration about this element.

About the Author

Nicole Williams learned about Charlotte Mason a few years after she began homeschooling and the same year, she added three additional students to her schoolroom! It was a trial by fire that resulted in a refinement of Charlotte Mason's methods and philosophy in her home. More than a decade later, she has written a living science curriculum, teaches at conferences, and co-hosts the Charlotte Mason podcast A Delectable Education. Nicole enjoys working in her garden, collecting living books, hiking, reading, and listening to podcasts.

Other Titles in This Series

Form 2 (Grades 4-6)
Astronomy. Find the Constellations by H.A. Rey
Botany. The First Book of Plants by Alice Dickinson
Chemistry. Matter, Molecules, and Atoms by Bertha Morris Parker
Engineering & Technology. The First Book of Machines by Walter Buehr
Geology. The First Book of the Earth by O. Irene Sevrey
Physics - Magnets. Magnets by Rocco V. Feravolo
Physics - Waves. The First Book of Sound by David Knight
Physics - Energy. The First Book of Electricity by Sam and Beryl Epstein
Weather. Rain, Hail, Sleet & Snow by Nancy Larrick

Form 3-4 (Grades 7-9)
Astronomy. The Planets by Dava Sobel
Biology. Men, Microscopes, and Living Things by Katherine B. Shippen
Botany. First Studies of Plant Life by George Francis Atkinson
Chemistry. The Mystery of the Periodic Table by Benjamin Wiker
Engineering & Technology. Electronics for Kids by Øyvind Nydal Dahl
Geology. Rocks, Rivers and the Changing Earth: A First Book About Geology by Herman and Nina Schneider
Physics. Secrets of the Universe by Paul Fleisher
Weather. Look at the Sky and Tell the Weather by Eric Sloane

High School (Grades 9-12)
Biology, Anatomy part 1. The Body: A Guide for Occupants by Bill Bryson
Biology, Anatomy part 2. The Body: A Guide for Occupants by Bill Bryson
Biology, Ecology. Creation Care: A Biblical Theology of the Natural World by Douglas J. Moo and Jonathan A. Moo
Chemistry, part 1. Wonders of Chemistry by A. Frederick Collins
Chemistry, part 2. Wonders of Chemistry by A. Frederick Collins
Chemistry, part 3. Wonders of Chemistry by A. Frederick Collins
Earth Science: Geology. Aerial Geography by Mary Caperton Morton
Earth Science: Weather. The Secret World of Weather by Tristan Gooley
Physics, part 1. For the Love of Physics by Walter Lewin
Physics, part 2. For the Love of Physics by Walter Lewin
Physics, part 3/Earth Science: Astrophysics. For the Love of Physics by Walter Lewin

Made in the USA
Monee, IL
15 August 2024

63893032R00040